Andrew's
ESSENTIAL
GUIDE TO BEGINNERS
GOLF

WELCOME TO THE ANDREW'S ESSENTIAL GUIDE TO BEGINNERS GOLF

The idea for the book came from Paul Furnival, a York businessman and a pupil of golf coach Andrew Smith. Andrew, the second member of the team, has been teaching golf at all levels for 30 years as a club professional and is now a full time coach. Paul noticed a shortage of easy to use, easy to understand, golf books for beginners. Peter Syson, a graphic designer from York, is the third member of the team. Peter is a keen 12-handicap golfer and his design experience brought another dimension to the book.

Andrew's speciality is teaching people to play golf quickly and efficiently. He is also a qualified rules official. Andrew draws on this vast experience and knowledge of all aspects of golf to make this book a golfer's companion.

With this unique blend of talent, The Andrew's Book Company was formed in 2004. The Andrew's Essential Guide to Beginners Golf is aimed at new players, but its refreshing simplicity will help players of all standards.

This book is all about taking the first steps in mastering the difficult game of golf. Through the use of simple illustrations, each section teaches you the basics of golf. They show how anyone, regardless of ability, can harness their enthusiasm for golf to be able to confidently hit the ball.

Happy Golfing

The Team
Andrew Smith
Peter Syson
Paul Furnival

THE ANDREW'S BOOK COMPANY

Copyright © The Andrew's Book Company

The right of The Andrew's Book Company to be identified as the author of this work has been asserted in accordance with the Copyright, Designs and Patents Act 1988

First published May 2005 by
The Andrew's Book Company

First reprint July 2008
Second reprint October 2011

CIP catalogue records for this book are available from the British Library.

ISBN 978-0-9550248-0-1

The Andrew's Book Company
156a Haxby Road, York YO31 8JN, United Kingdom
Tel 01904 639944
Email info@andrewsgolf.co.uk
www.andrewsgolf.co.uk

Designed and produced by Rubber Band Graphic Design, York, UK
www.rubberband-design.co.uk

INTRODUCTION

Golf can be a challenging game to play as a beginner. What you can do, is learn a few basics to help you achieve a reasonable standard of play and golf knowledge.

That's where Andrew's Essential Guide to Beginners Golf can help. This book is an impressive step-by-step guide on the basics of how to play the game, a few rules, course etiquette, what equipment to buy and how to score. From never holding a golf club before, you will very quickly learn how to get the ball moving forward to an adequate level of distance and accuracy.

Consistent golf is all about setting yourself up correctly to hit the ball and understanding how the swing works. To simplify instructions we have dispensed with jargon and used illustrative drawings to show basic techniques to practice.

In the book you will learn:

- How to hold a golf club
- How to aim at the target
- The correct posture
- The half swing
- The full swing
- What equipment to buy
- About a golf course
- Basic rules
- How to score and the function of the golf handicap
- About a score card

Andrew's

golf.co.uk

"

A journey of
a thousand
leagues
begins with
a single step

"

Chinese Proverb

CONTENTS

SECTION 4 LET'S PLAY GOLF

SECTION 5 BASIC RULES

SECTION 6 COMPETITIONS

TIPS, DID YOU KNOW & ETIQUETTE RUNNING THROUGHOUT THE BOOK.

TIP

To help with understanding your golf swing – try to see a reflection of yourself in a window or a mirror.

DID YOU KNOW?

A player has "addressed the ball" when taken a stance and the club grounded.

ETIQUETTE

No player should play until the players in front are out of range.

Andrew's

golf.co.uk

GRIP

GRIP ... the essential ingredient for control of the clubface

Learn how to hold the golf club correctly

The grip is a basic essential to achieving elements of a controlled golf swing.
For the purposes of learning to play golf, use a 7 or 8 iron.

Rest the bottom of the club on the ground and pinch the top of the grip with the forefinger and thumb of the right hand, (this is to keep the club in position), and **aim** the bottom of the clubface at the target.

Stretch open the left hand and make the back of your hand face the target. Now bring the left hand towards the grip. Your hand must touch the club across the base of the fingers. **(see inset i)**. Wrap the hand around the golf club so that the fleshy part of the hand sits on the front of the golf club. The pad of the left thumb must be pressed onto the front of the club and be slightly right of centre.

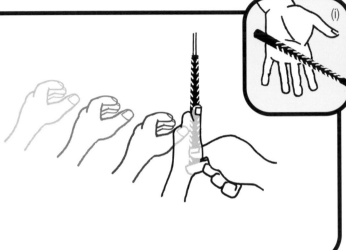

Overlapping Grip

The right hand now approaches the golf club with the palm facing the target and will sit below the left. The golf club sits in the fingers of the right hand with the little finger of the right hand overlapping the forefinger of the left hand **(see inset ii)**. Finally wrap right hand over left thumb with the right thumb touching the right forefinger.

Interlocking Grip

As above but instead of overlapping the little finger of the right hand with the forefinger of the left, interlock them **(see inset iii)**.

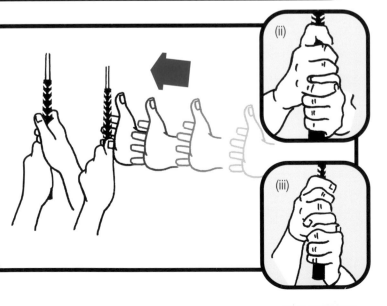

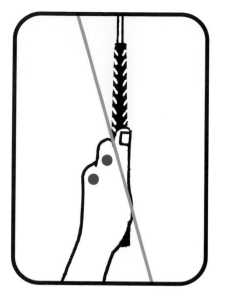

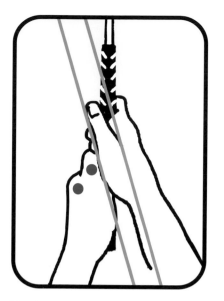

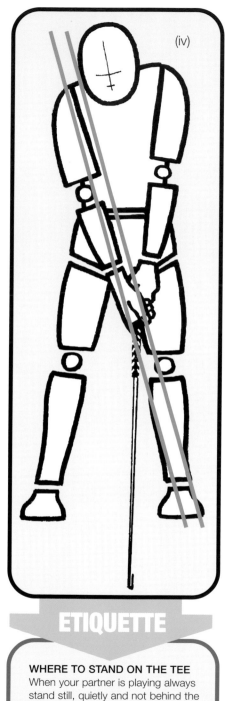

(iv)

When you look down at your left hand you should be able to see two knuckles. If you can only see one knuckle then your left hand is too far to the left, and if you can see three knuckles then your left hand is too far to the right.

The lines formed between the forefingers and thumbs, indicated in blue on the illustration, should point to the middle of your right shoulder **(see inset iv)**.

DID YOU KNOW?

The reason for a glove

To improve strength, stability and grip in the left hand.

The glove is normally worn on one hand – the left hand, or right hand for left handed players. Gloves are manufactured in leather or synthetic or a combination of the two.

TIP
IMPORTANT

When buying a glove make sure it is a tight fit.

TIP

For correct position of club in left hand, mark your glove with a pen where your club should lie.

ETIQUETTE

WHERE TO STAND ON THE TEE
When your partner is playing always stand still, quietly and not behind the ball.

15

Andrew's

golf.co.uk

AIM

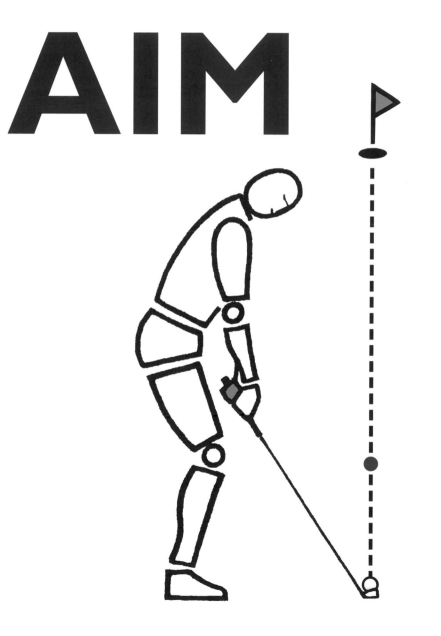

AIM ... the club not the eyes

Learn how to aim the clubhead at the target

Aim and alignment is a discipline in golf often not given enough attention.
Learn to aim and develop a routine to stay with you.

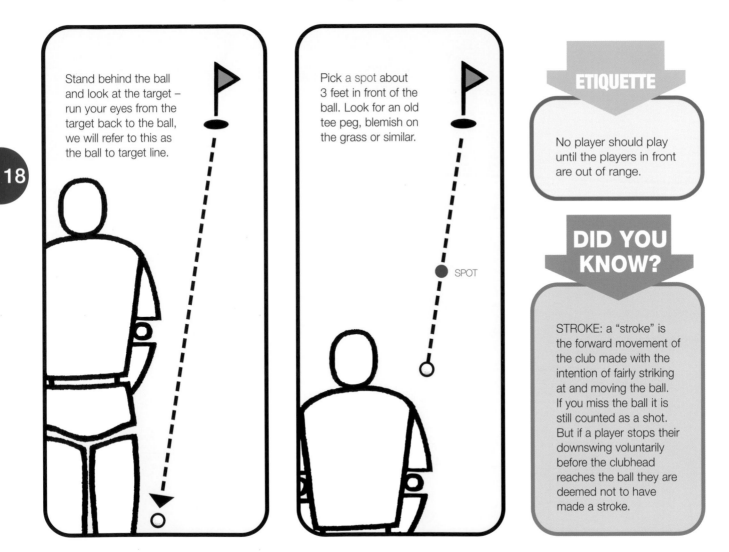

Stand behind the ball and look at the target – run your eyes from the target back to the ball, we will refer to this as the ball to target line.

Pick a spot about 3 feet in front of the ball. Look for an old tee peg, blemish on the grass or similar.

SPOT

ETIQUETTE

No player should play until the players in front are out of range.

DID YOU KNOW?

STROKE: a "stroke" is the forward movement of the club made with the intention of fairly striking at and moving the ball. If you miss the ball it is still counted as a shot. But if a player stops their downswing voluntarily before the clubhead reaches the ball they are deemed not to have made a stroke.

Now stand sideways to the ball to target line and place the clubhead behind the ball at 90° to the ball to target line. In other words, aim the clubhead at the spot 3 feet in front of the ball – it is a lot easier to aim at a close target than a distant one.

SPOT

Aiming the club correctly is crucial as a few degrees out at address will be many yards at the target.

SPOT ON!

Clubface open at address.
Aiming right of the target.

Clubface closed at address.
Aiming left of the target.

TIP

By standing behind the ball, you will familiarise yourself with the ball to target line which will be useful when aligning your body at address.

Andrew's
golf.co.uk

POSTURE

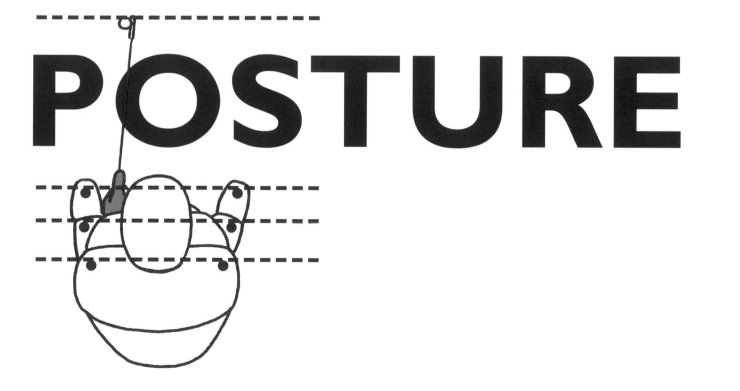

POSTURE

... the foundation of a successful golf swing

How to stand when preparing to hit the ball

Set up position for ball and club distance.

As we are learning to play with a 7 or 8 iron, then the ideal ball position is halfway between the centre of the stance and the inside of the left foot. At address the hands should be slightly ahead of the ball.

We will stay with this ball position whilst learning the swing.

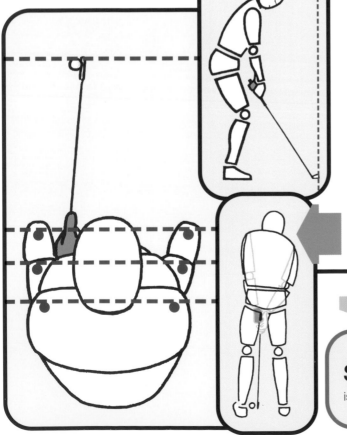

ALIGNMENT

Now that we have the correct **grip** of the golf club and are able to **aim** the clubface at the target our next step is to align our body to achieve a correct stance.

Simply, the feet, knees, hips and shoulders must be on a line parallel to the ball to target line.

Back view showing the ideal ball position and the right shoulder tilted below the left (because your right hand is below your left).

DID YOU KNOW?

A player has "addressed the ball" when a stance has been taken and the club grounded.

ETIQUETTE

Safety Prior to playing a stroke or making a practice swing, the player should ensure that no one is standing close by or in a position to be hit by the club.

Simple steps to perfect posture

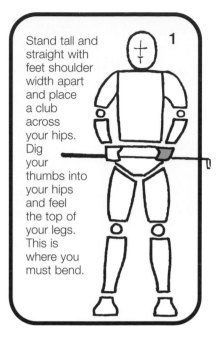

1 Stand tall and straight with feet shoulder width apart and place a club across your hips. Dig your thumbs into your hips and feel the top of your legs. This is where you must bend.

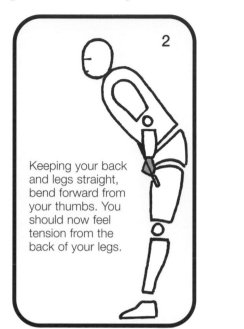

2 Keeping your back and legs straight, bend forward from your thumbs. You should now feel tension from the back of your legs.

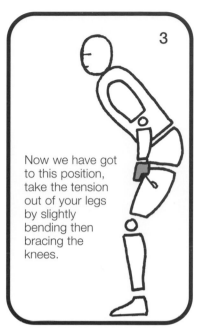

3 Now we have got to this position, take the tension out of your legs by slightly bending then bracing the knees.

4 Still holding the golf club, let your arms fall forward and hang freely from the shoulders.

5 This is the correct position for your body. Now referring back to **aim, grip, alignment,** you are now ready to start the backswing.

TIP
To check your correct distance away from the ball, providing you have assumed the right posture, then a good test is to place the grip end of the club on your left leg, it should now rest approximately 2" to 3" above the left knee.

2" – 3" above knee

TIP

Improve your posture by practising pictures 1–5 using a golf club, broom handle, or similar alternative everyday in your work and home.

Andrew's

golf.co.uk

HALF SWING

HALF SWING

... the foundation of a full golf swing

The key to a good swing is the first movement of the club backwards away from the ball

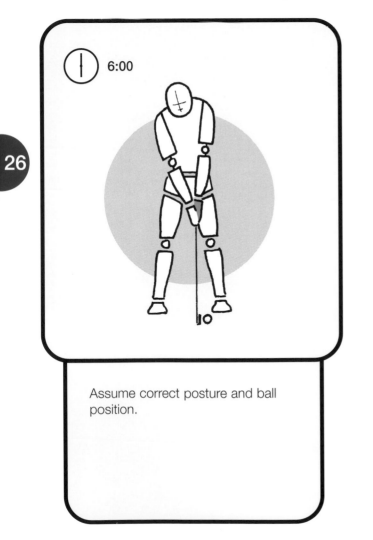

6:00

Assume correct posture and ball position.

8:00

Focus on turning the club, your arms, your shoulders and stomach away from the ball. At this stage keep your lower body and hips fairly still.

Reasons for learning a half swing

When learning to play golf, the half swing should be regularly practised to build confidence before moving onto the full swing.

The idea is to be able to competently hit the ball straight and get the ball airborne.

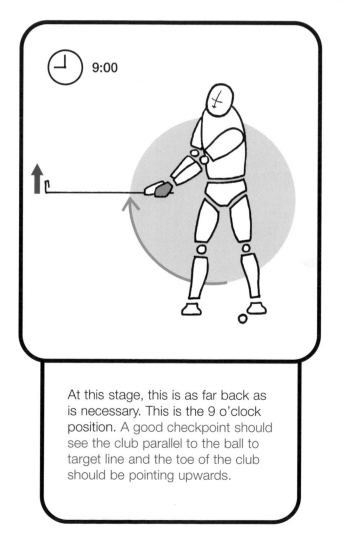

At this stage, this is as far back as is necessary. This is the 9 o'clock position. A good checkpoint should see the club parallel to the ball to target line and the toe of the club should be pointing upwards.

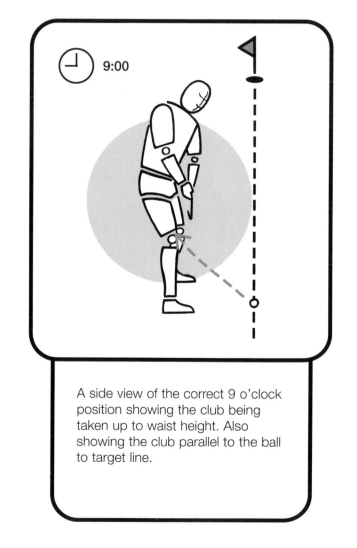

A side view of the correct 9 o'clock position showing the club being taken up to waist height. Also showing the club parallel to the ball to target line.

HALF SWING
... down swing

TIP

To help with your down swing and follow through imagine you are throwing a bucket of water.

🕗 8:00

Whilst keeping your eye on the ball, start the down swing by simply pulling the back of the left hand towards the ball. At the same time rotate your body towards the ball.

🕕 6:00

At impact your weight should now have transferred onto your left side, eyes still looking at the ball.

HALF SWING
... follow through

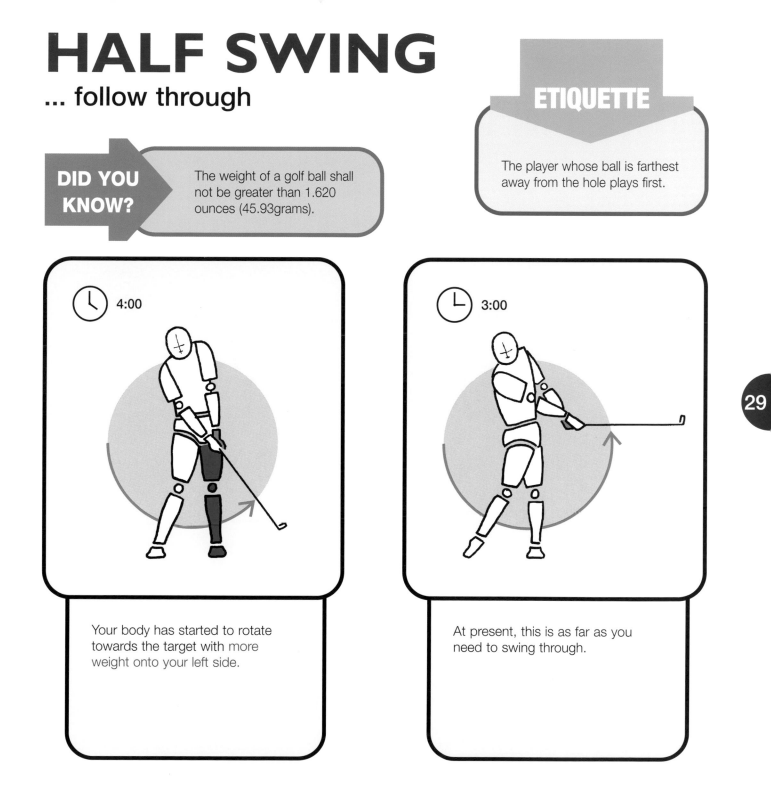

DID YOU KNOW?

The weight of a golf ball shall not be greater than 1.620 ounces (45.93grams).

ETIQUETTE

The player whose ball is farthest away from the hole plays first.

🕓 4:00

Your body has started to rotate towards the target with more weight onto your left side.

🕓 3:00

At present, this is as far as you need to swing through.

Andrew's

golf.co.uk

FULL SWING

FULL SWING

... take it to the top

A good full swing requires a 90° shoulder turn

The foundation of the half swing on the previous pages will take you on to the full swing which is merely an extension of the half swing.

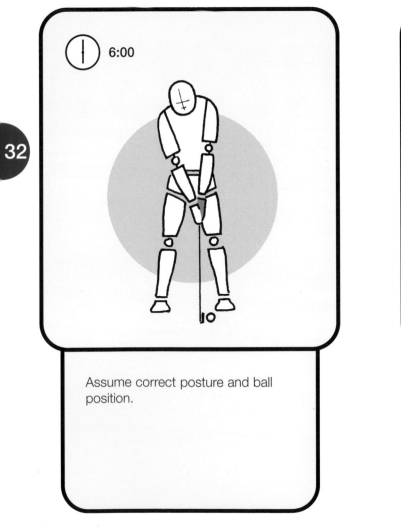

6:00

Assume correct posture and ball position.

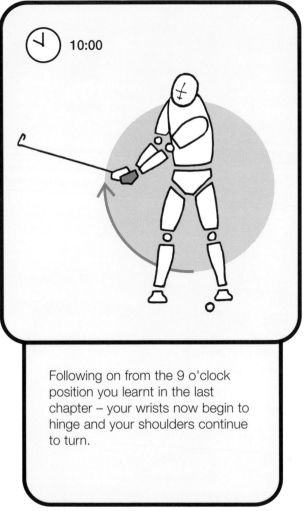

10:00

Following on from the 9 o'clock position you learnt in the last chapter – your wrists now begin to hinge and your shoulders continue to turn.

FULL SWING
... at the top

12:00

Moving from 9 o'clock your wrists continue to hinge and take the club upwards and behind your head. Your right knee must remain flexed.
At the top of your back swing:
- shoulders have turned 90°
- hips have turned 45°

11:00

Start the down swing by pulling your left hand and arm towards the ball. Your body has started to turn towards the ball.

FULL SWING
... impact

TIP

To help with understanding your golf swing try to see a reflection of yourself in a window or a mirror.

34

| 6:00

Your left arm continues to pull towards the ball. Your body rotates to increase power ready for the hit. At impact the ball is struck with a descending blow (loft will lift the ball – see equipment page). Your weight is mainly on your left side.

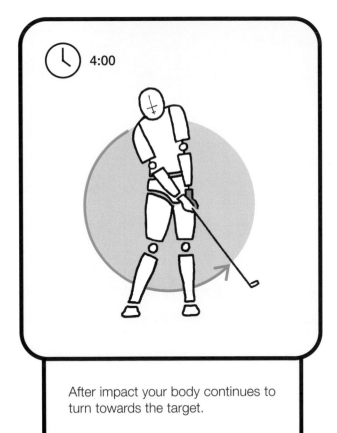

🕓 4:00

After impact your body continues to turn towards the target.

FULL SWING
... the finish

Now is the time to put together all you have learnt

GRIP	✔
AIM	✔
POSTURE	✔
HALF SWING	✔
FULL SWING... READ ON	

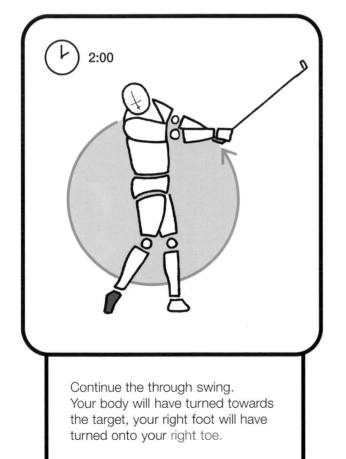

🕐 2:00

Continue the through swing.
Your body will have turned towards the target, your right foot will have turned onto your right toe.

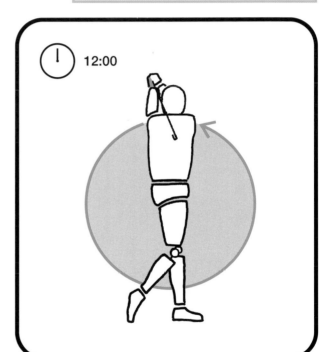

🕛 12:00

The final position
Your body has turned fully to face the target. Your finish is balanced. A player with the correct through swing will be able to hold this finish position.

FULL SWING

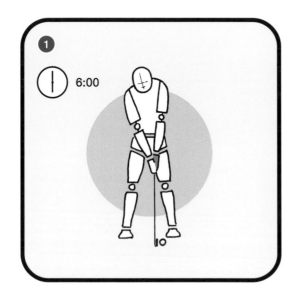

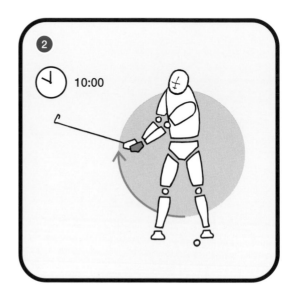

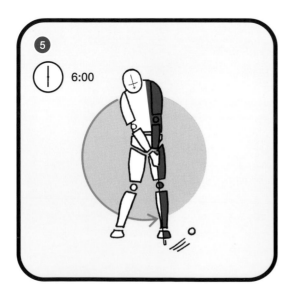

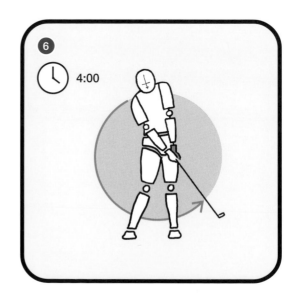

... now put it all together

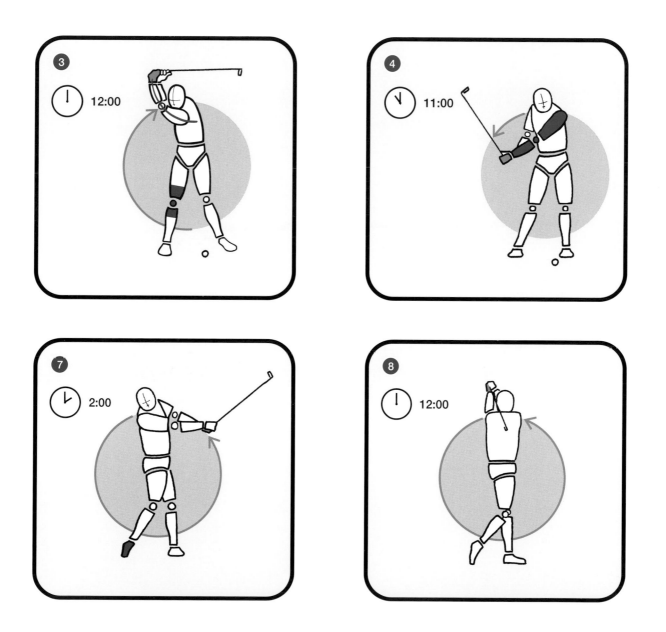

Andrew's

golf.co.uk

SPINE ANGLE

SPINE ANGLE

... vital for stability in a golf swing

The benefits of a constant spine angle are that it helps keep the head still and the club on the correct swing plane

It is essential to keep a constant body angle to the ground all the way through a golf swing. The following visuals demonstrate the correct spine angle throughout a golf swing.

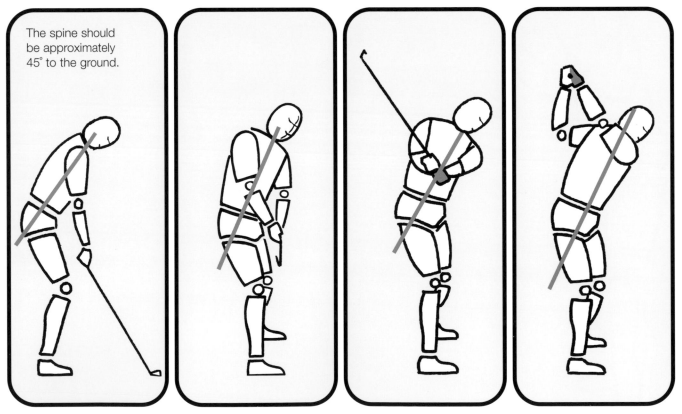

The spine should be approximately 45° to the ground.

As seen in the above pictures, the spine remains in a constant position – eyes looking at the ball.

TIP

To help understand swing plane imagine a line drawn from your shoulder to the ball – you must swing the club underneath this line at all times.

DID YOU KNOW?

'FORE' comes from the word 'forecaddie' who were employed by players in the 19th century to indicate the position of the ball – balls in those days were extremely expensive and the forecaddie was expected to find the ball.

If your ball is heading towards another player yell 'FORE' as quickly and loudly as possible to alert them of the danger.

If you hear 'FORE' quickly cover your head and duck.

ETIQUETTE

A divot is a piece of turf taken out of the ground when striking the ball.

The divot must be picked up, replaced and pressed down with your foot. This will allow the grass to grow back.

Only at the finish do you start to straighten up!

Andrew's

golf.co.uk

EXERCISE TO ROTATE

EXERCISE TO ROTATE

... to help create a full shoulder turn

As previously learnt you must maintain the spine angle you have created with the correct posture.

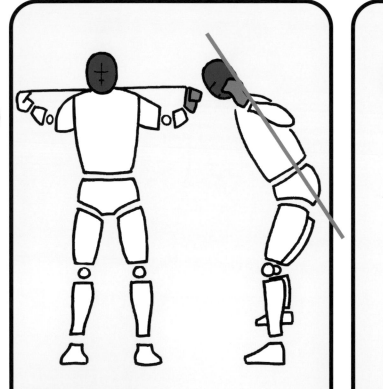

Place a club behind your shoulders and maintain your spine angle. It is important to keep your head still and your eyes looking at the ball throughout this exercise.

Rotate your shoulders to the right, feel resistance in your flexed right knee, keep turning, this will stretch your upper body to a full powerful back swing position.

TIP

Do this exercise five times in the morning and five times in the evening to help increase your flexibility.

DID YOU KNOW?

If a group is holding up the players behind and has lost more than a hole on the players in front, it should invite the players behind to play through.

Whilst still looking at the ball, unwind your body and start to turn towards the target.

Finish with your stomach facing the target and your weight on your left side and up on your right toe.

Andrew's

golf.co.uk

SLOPING LIES

SLOPING LIES

... learning the correct way to stand

The key to coping with uphill and downhill lies is at the address

Golf courses are not always flat. Prepare yourself for sloping lies with this simple drill.

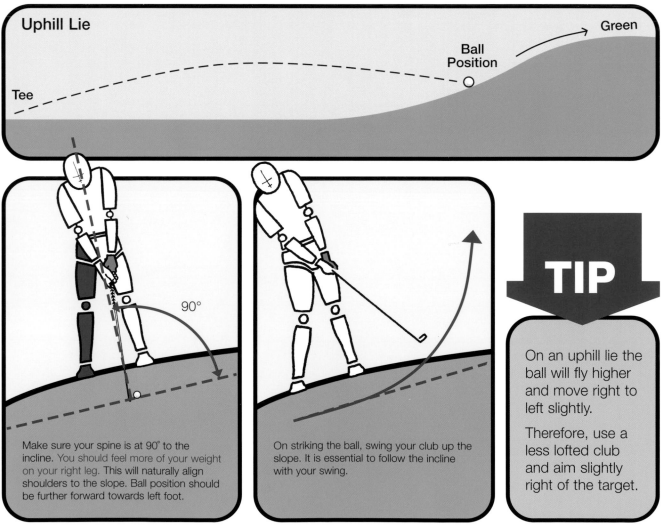

Uphill Lie

Tee

Ball Position

Green

90°

Make sure your spine is at 90° to the incline. You should feel more of your weight on your right leg. This will naturally align shoulders to the slope. Ball position should be further forward towards left foot.

On striking the ball, swing your club up the slope. It is essential to follow the incline with your swing.

TIP

On an uphill lie the ball will fly higher and move right to left slightly.

Therefore, use a less lofted club and aim slightly right of the target.

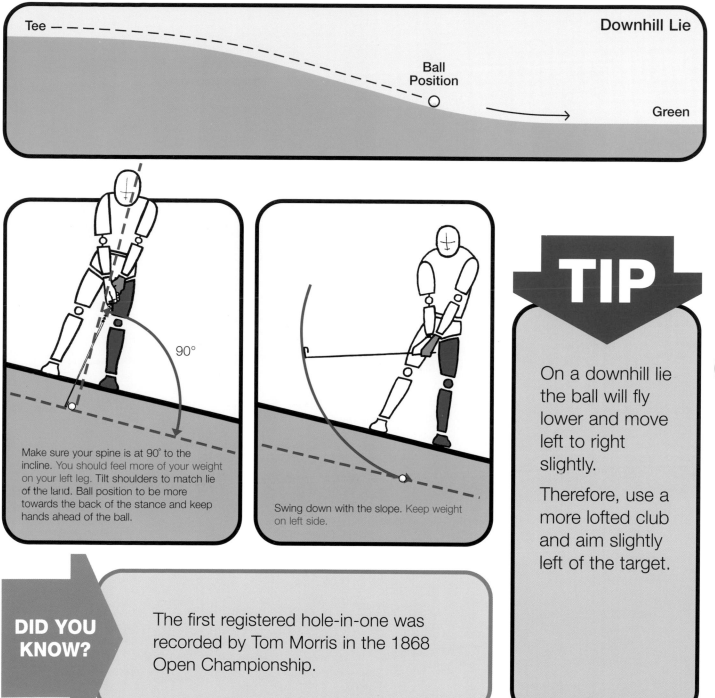

Tee

Downhill Lie

Ball Position

Green

90°

Make sure your spine is at 90° to the incline. You should feel more of your weight on your left leg. Tilt shoulders to match lie of the land. Ball position to be more towards the back of the stance and keep hands ahead of the ball.

Swing down with the slope. Keep weight on left side.

TIP

On a downhill lie the ball will fly lower and move left to right slightly.

Therefore, use a more lofted club and aim slightly left of the target.

DID YOU KNOW?

The first registered hole-in-one was recorded by Tom Morris in the 1868 Open Championship.

49

Andrew's
golf.co.uk

EQUIPMENT

EQUIPMENT

... what clubs do you need?

A basic guide to clubs and their uses

Woods

So called because they were originally made from wood. Now made from steel, titanium or a mixture of graphite and titanium.

Club	Uses		Lofts
Driver or 1 Wood	Driving from the tee		Available from 6° to 12°. As a beginner 11° is more suitable and easier to control
3 Wood	Driving from the tee and off the fairway		Available 12° to 14°
5 Wood	Predominantly off the fairway but can be used from the tee		Available 17° to 19°
7 Wood	Fairway use and light rough. Can be used from the tee		Available 20° to 22°
Rescue Wood	Hybrid between a wood and an iron. To be used instead of 3 or 4 iron		

Irons and Putters

Club	Uses		Loft	Lie Angle	Club Length
3	Distance iron from fairway or tee		21°	59°	39"
4	Distance iron from fairway or tee		24°	60°	38.5"
5	Mid-iron from fairway and tee with more accuracy		27°	61°	38"
6	Mid-iron from fairway and light rough		30°	62°	37.5"
7	Mid-iron from fairway and light to heavy rough, chip and run		34°	62.5°	37"
8	Short iron used on fairway for accurate shots to green, rough, chip and run		38°	63°	36.5"
9	Short iron for accurate high trajectory shots, from heavy rough, chipping around green		42°	63.5°	36"
PW	Pitching wedge for pitch shots to green, from heavy rough, chipping around green		47°	64°	35.5"
SW	Sand wedge, predominantly used out of bunkers, short pitch shots, chipping around green, getting out of high rough		55°	64.5°	35.25"
Putter	For use on the putting green. Can also be used from off the putting green as it can sometimes be easier to use than chipping the ball. Unlimited designs and lengths available. Try before you buy.				

Golf Club Definitions

SHAFT
LIE ANGLE
TOE
HEEL

SHAFT
LOFT
HOSEL
FACE
SOLE

53

TIP

Shafts are made in different flexes. Soft shafts (ladies + 'A' flex) are for slower swing speeds, 'R' flex (regular) are for average players, 'S' flex (stiff) are for players with fast swings. XS for tournament pro's.

ETIQUETTE

To avoid confusion, mark your golf ball with a pen. This will firmly establish that the ball you are about to play is yours.

Club trajectory and approximate distances

For ladies deduct about 20% off the distances – otherwise everything else applies.

Woods

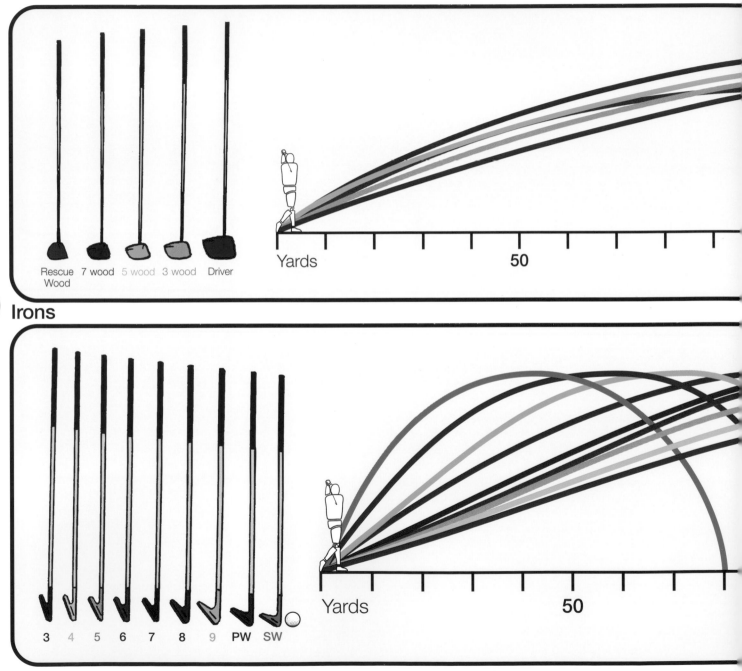

Rescue Wood   7 wood   5 wood   3 wood   Driver

Yards   50

Irons

3   4   5   6   7   8   9   PW   SW

Yards   50

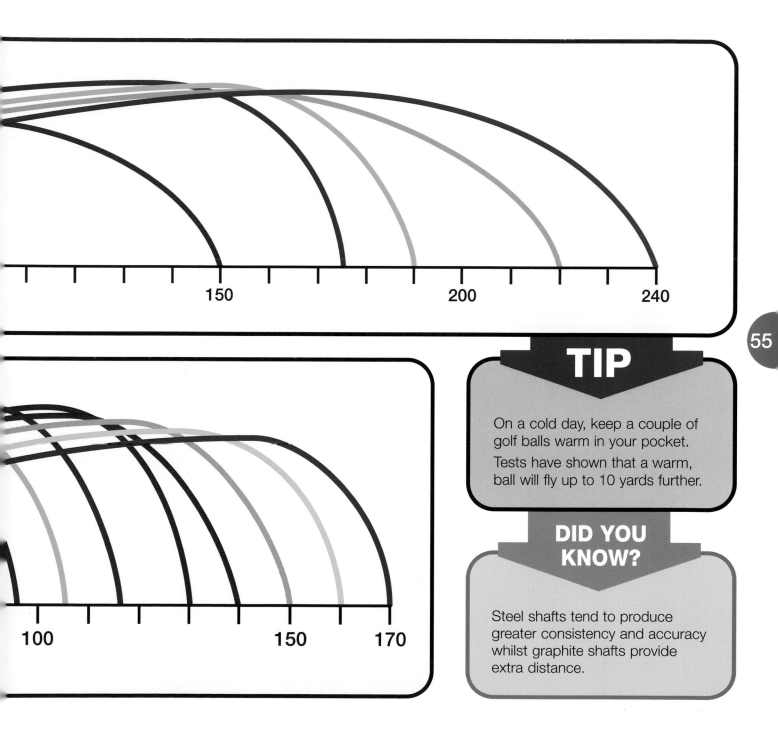

TIP

On a cold day, keep a couple of golf balls warm in your pocket.

Tests have shown that a warm, ball will fly up to 10 yards further.

DID YOU KNOW?

Steel shafts tend to produce greater consistency and accuracy whilst graphite shafts provide extra distance.

EQUIPMENT

... what do you need?
A guide to basic equipment and their uses

Clubs

Players may have many different combinations of golf clubs in their golf bags.

Each club is designed to hit the ball a certain height and distance – See charts on pages 54 and 55.

Lower Number Clubs

As shown on the charts, clubs get longer and their loft decreases as their numbers decrease.

- In short – lower number – longer shots, on landing the ball will run.
  Higher number – higher shots, on landing the ball will stop quicker.

- After a little practice you will find out more about each club.

- As a beginner a full set is not always necessary. A driver is difficult to use, it maybe easier to try a 3 or 5 wood from the tee.

Higher Number Clubs

- On the fairway use a 5 or 7 iron and then a 9, PW or sand iron for lofting the ball onto the green.

- Use a sand iron out of bunkers and finally use a putter on the green to putt the ball into the hole.

Balls

As a beginner, differences in golf balls do not matter. Some balls are harder so go a bit further but produce less backspin. Softer balls don't go quite as far, but produce more backspin allowing the ball to stop quickly on the green.

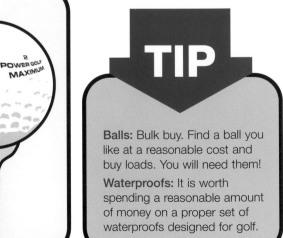

Balls come in three colours as follows:

- White – most popular

- Optic yellow – easier to see

- Optic orange – easier to see in snow/frost

The name on a ball is the manufacturers and their brand. Also there will be a number, which helps identify your ball.

Tee Pegs

These are designed to elevate your ball on the teeing ground. Only to be used on the tee not on the fairway. Wood or plastic. It's up to you.

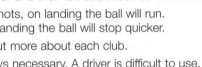

TIP

Balls: Bulk buy. Find a ball you like at a reasonable cost and buy loads. You will need them!

Waterproofs: It is worth spending a reasonable amount of money on a proper set of waterproofs designed for golf.

Shoes

A good fitting comfortable pair of shoes is essential. It can be 4 miles around an 18 hole course – more if you don't play in a straight line. Golf shoes have spikes on the sole, either metal or rubber, to increase your stability whilst playing a shot and also to keep feet dry and prevent slipping on damp grass.

Prices and colours vary, it's your choice.

Clothing

Wear whatever you are comfortable in and in winter wear warm waterproof clothing with room to move/swing. The main no-no is denim jeans. Denim jeans are not permitted at most private golf clubs.

At driving ranges and pay and play courses wear what you like.

ETIQUETTE

When playing on or near the putting green leave your bag or trolley near to the exit to the next tee.

DID YOU KNOW?

Golf clubs bought off the shelf are for people of average height. Shorter or taller people will need the lie angle altering and possibly the shaft may need shortening or lengthening.

Grips may also be made thicker or thinner depending on your hand size.

Get advice from your expert.

Bags and Trolleys

Bags

Bags can be carried or wheeled around on a trolley – you decide.

- Carry bags have a dual strap to fit over both shoulders to distribute the weight.

- Trolley bags are often larger and more rigid. They have loads of pockets that can carry everything from car keys to waterproof clothing.

Worth noting: Golf courses will often have a trolley ban in the winter to protect the course. Be prepared, you may wish to buy a light carry bag just for winter play.

Trolleys

Manual pull trolley or battery driven electric.

Andrew's
golf.co.uk

THE COURSE

THE COURSE

- Golf is played on a course over 18 'holes'.
- Some golf courses are only 9 holes or even 6 holes.
- Generally golf courses with 9 or 6 holes are played 2 or 3 times to make a full round of 18 holes.
- The idea of golf is to tee off on the teeing ground of hole No.1, play towards the green of hole No.1 and get the ball into the hole in as few strokes as possible.
- A 'hole' consists of a teeing ground (where you start from), a green (where you finish) and a fairway – in between the teeing ground and the green.
- A fairway is short cut grass between the tee and the green.

Out of Bounds

Rough

Semi Rough

Mens Tee

Ladies Tee

Fairway

- To create more interest the green is often undulating.
- Somewhere on the green a hole will be cut that measures 4 ¼" (108mm) across.
- A flagstick will be placed in the hole to indicate its position.

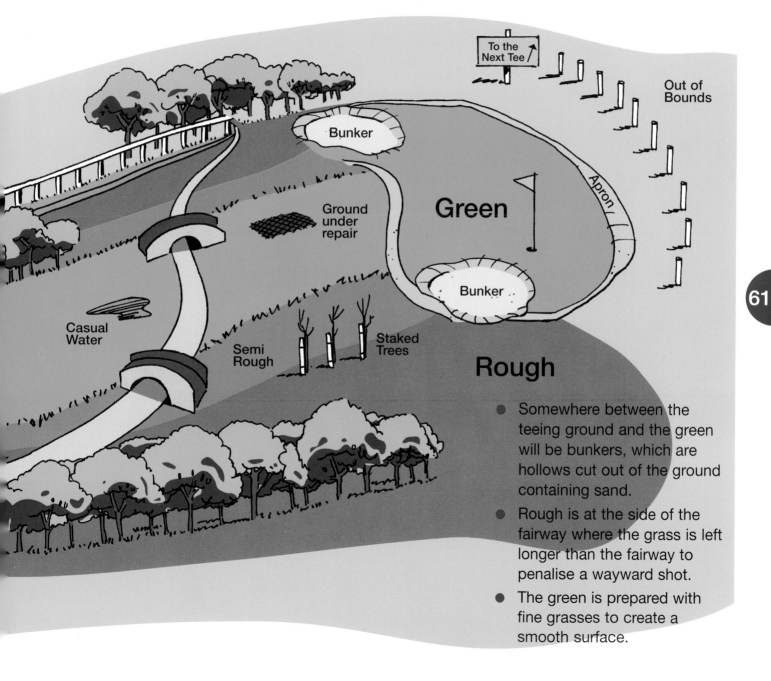

To the Next Tee

Out of Bounds

Bunker

Ground under repair

Green

Apron

Casual Water

Bunker

Semi Rough

Staked Trees

Rough

- Somewhere between the teeing ground and the green will be bunkers, which are hollows cut out of the ground containing sand.
- Rough is at the side of the fairway where the grass is left longer than the fairway to penalise a wayward shot.
- The green is prepared with fine grasses to create a smooth surface.

61

Andrew's

golf.co.uk

LET'S PLAY GOLF

LET'S PLAY GOLF

Referring to the course, start on the first tee

What is 'PAR'?

The number of strokes a first-class golfer should normally require for a hole or course.

Par 5
475 yards +

3 shots
2 putts

Par 4
250 – 474 yards

2 shots
2 putts

Par 3
0 – 249 yards

1 shot
2 putts

TEE

TEE

TEE

Where do I tee the ball?

Coloured markers will be set out on the tee:

- ● Red for ladies
- ○ Yellow for men
- ○ White for men's competition play.

Place your ball between the markers anywhere in the hatched area.

Direction of play →

2 Club Lengths

Teeing up

Hold the ball on your tee peg and push the peg into the ground as shown.

Make sure the ball is not in front of the markers and no more than 2 club lengths behind the markers.

How high should I tee the ball?

The general rule of thumb, is when you place your club on the ground behind the ball, about ½ to ¾ of the ball should be showing above the clubface.

½ to ¾

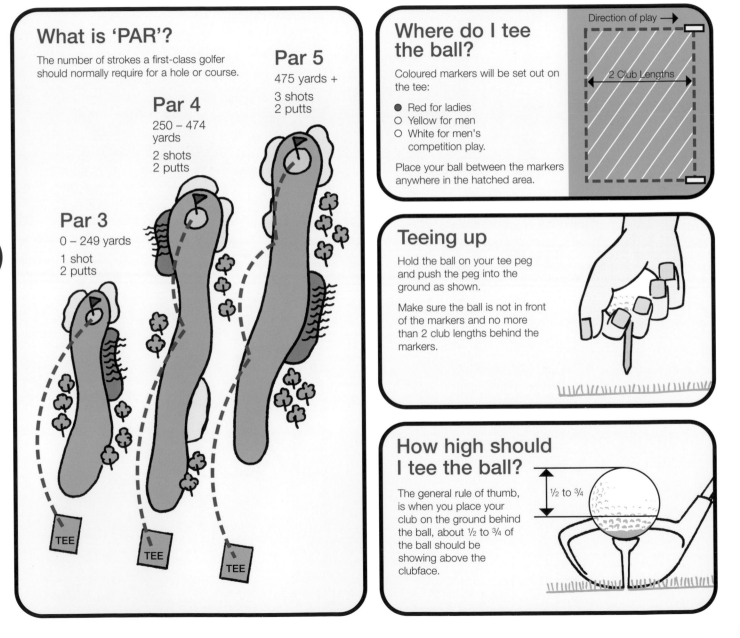

You are now in a position to play your first shot. Select the club according to the distance charts in the equipment section and drive the ball from the tee.

Where do I position the ball in relation to my stance?

Longer Clubs

Shorter Clubs

As shown in the diagram: Longer clubs towards the left foot and shorter clubs towards the centre. Longer clubs require a slightly wider stance.

Once on the fairway continue down towards the green selecting the clubs for correct distances. As a guide there will be distance markers, particularly 150 yard markers, from the green.

DID YOU KNOW?

You can stand outside the teeing area but your ball must be within it.

Recovery shots
from the rough

Use a lofted club (8 or 9 iron, wedge or sand iron), play the ball back in your stance towards your right foot. The ball must be struck with a descending blow. Aim to get the ball back onto the fairway.

TIP

Chip shots Keep it simple!

Swing the club back 1/3. Follow through 2/3.

Chip shots from the edge of the green

Looking at the diagrams the easiest shot to play is a 6 or 8 iron chip and run. If you have a mound or bunker to go over then use a more lofted club.

6 Iron

8 Iron

Chip & Run

Wedge

Sand Iron

Lob

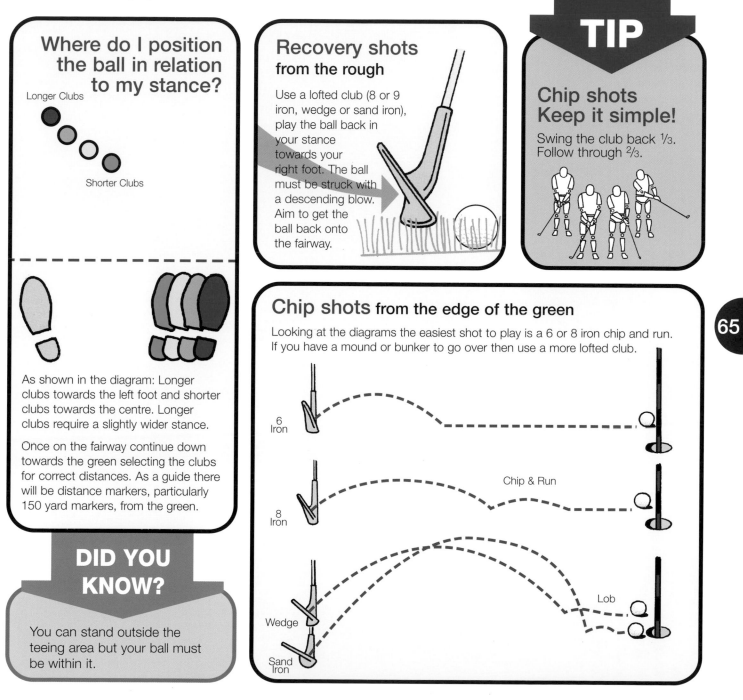

Bunker Shots
First of all you need to know a few bunker rules

- You must not ground your club in the bunker prior to playing your shot.
- You must not touch the sand on the back swing.
- Penalty for doing the above – 2 shots.

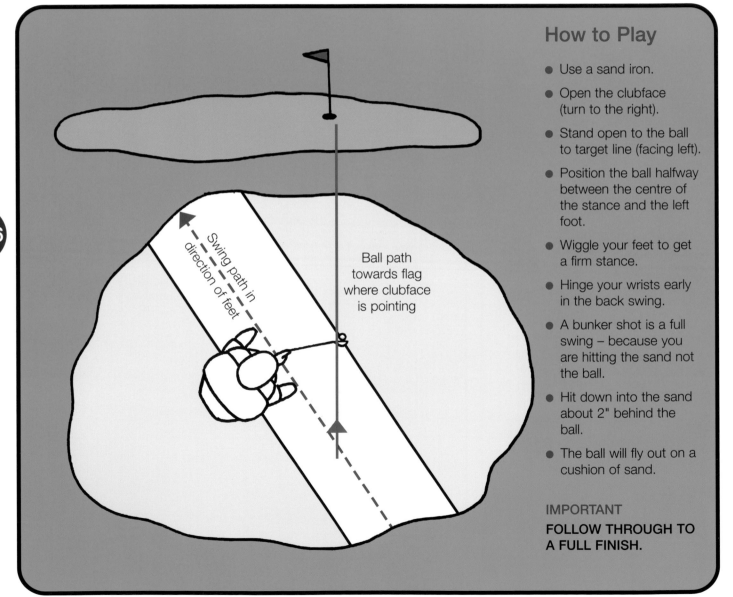

How to Play

- Use a sand iron.
- Open the clubface (turn to the right).
- Stand open to the ball to target line (facing left).
- Position the ball halfway between the centre of the stance and the left foot.
- Wiggle your feet to get a firm stance.
- Hinge your wrists early in the back swing.
- A bunker shot is a full swing – because you are hitting the sand not the ball.
- Hit down into the sand about 2" behind the ball.
- The ball will fly out on a cushion of sand.

IMPORTANT

FOLLOW THROUGH TO A FULL FINISH.

Swing path in direction of feet

Ball path towards flag where clubface is pointing

An open clubface is pointing to the right. To get the feel of an 'open' face try and balance a bottle on the clubface.

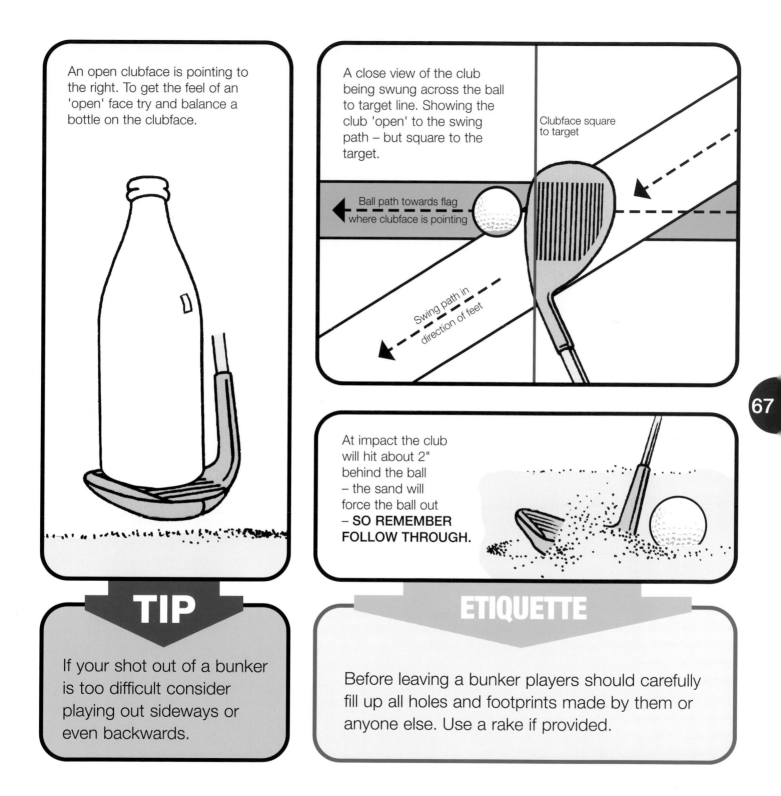

A close view of the club being swung across the ball to target line. Showing the club 'open' to the swing path – but square to the target.

Clubface square to target

Ball path towards flag where clubface is pointing

Swing path in direction of feet

At impact the club will hit about 2" behind the ball – the sand will force the ball out – **SO REMEMBER FOLLOW THROUGH.**

TIP

If your shot out of a bunker is too difficult consider playing out sideways or even backwards.

ETIQUETTE

Before leaving a bunker players should carefully fill up all holes and footprints made by them or anyone else. Use a rake if provided.

Putting
A putting green is a specially prepared surface of very short grass

A few rules you need to know

If your ball is on the putting green you may mark its position by placing a small coin or ball marker directly behind, you may then lift the ball to clean it.

The apron is the band of grass around the putting green where the grass is slightly longer. You may not mark your ball on this area.

If your ball is in the path of your partners putt, then you may be asked to mark your ball.

To replace your ball after marking, place the ball back on the green in exactly the same position and lift the marker.

When putting on the putting surface the flag must be taken out or attended. An attended flag is where your partner will hold the flag and lift it out of the hole as your ball approaches.

If your ball strikes the flag, it is a 2 stroke penalty.

How to putt

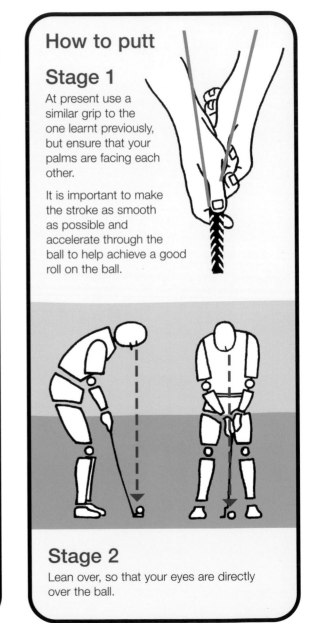

Stage 1

At present use a similar grip to the one learnt previously, but ensure that your palms are facing each other.

It is important to make the stroke as smooth as possible and accelerate through the ball to help achieve a good roll on the ball.

Stage 2

Lean over, so that your eyes are directly over the ball.

How to putt – Stage 3

The ball position should be forward in your stance towards your left foot. This will help create an ideal strike which is a slightly upward motion – one that catches the ball just above halfway and sets the ball rolling end over end with top spin.

Dominate the putting action from your shoulders making it a pendulum type stroke.

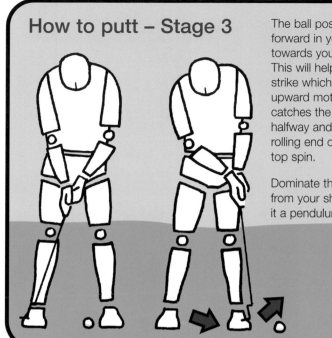

DID YOU KNOW?

A 'pitch mark' is an indentation on the green made by a golf ball.

TIP

Always repair your pitch mark and any more on the green by using a small metal fork called a pitch mark repairer (on sale in your local golf shop).

ETIQUETTE

Do not take your bag or trolley onto the green.

69

A drill to help create a smooth putting action

Adopt your putting stance, then trap another club against your chest. Keeping the club in place try rock your right shoulder up and down to move the putter back and through. This will help keep the arms and shoulders as one complete unit and will create a good smooth action, not a wristy flick at the ball. You will now stroke the ball with an upward movement creating top spin.

Reading a Green

Most putting greens have some kind of slope. To help see a slope stand back from the ball and assess the severity of the slope.

Andrew's

golf.co.uk

BASIC RULES

BASIC RULES

... what happens if?

A brief guide to some rules you need to know

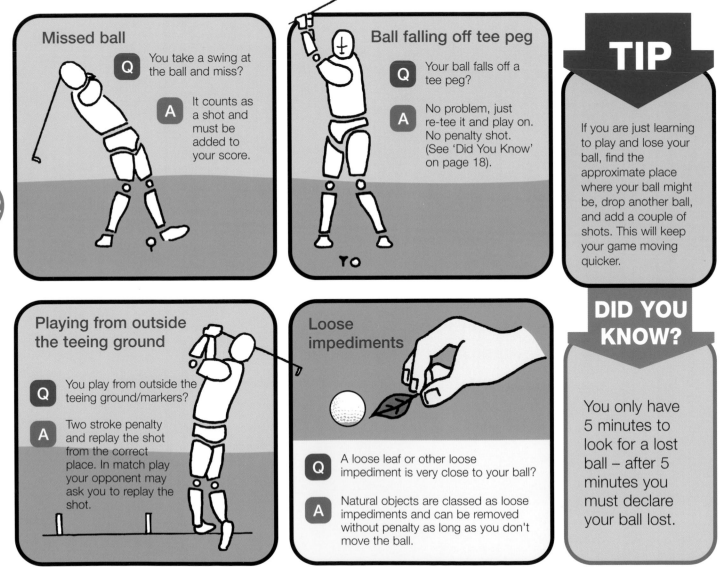

Missed ball

Q You take a swing at the ball and miss?

A It counts as a shot and must be added to your score.

Ball falling off tee peg

Q Your ball falls off a tee peg?

A No problem, just re-tee it and play on. No penalty shot. (See 'Did You Know' on page 18).

Playing from outside the teeing ground

Q You play from outside the teeing ground/markers?

A Two stroke penalty and replay the shot from the correct place. In match play your opponent may ask you to replay the shot.

Loose impediments

Q A loose leaf or other loose impediment is very close to your ball?

A Natural objects are classed as loose impediments and can be removed without penalty as long as you don't move the ball.

TIP

If you are just learning to play and lose your ball, find the approximate place where your ball might be, drop another ball, and add a couple of shots. This will keep your game moving quicker.

DID YOU KNOW?

You only have 5 minutes to look for a lost ball – after 5 minutes you must declare your ball lost.

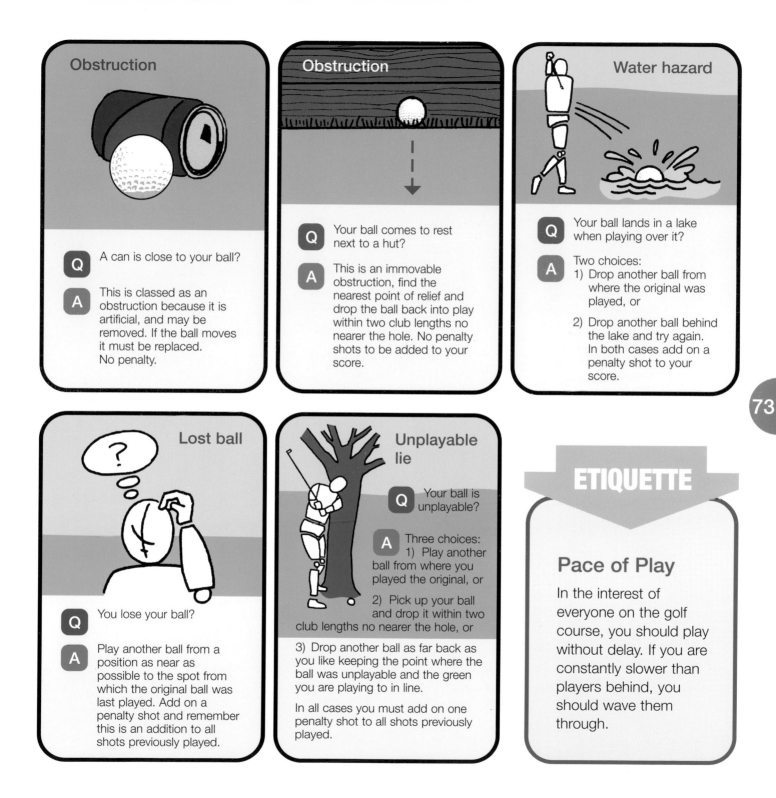

Obstruction

Q A can is close to your ball?

A This is classed as an obstruction because it is artificial, and may be removed. If the ball moves it must be replaced. No penalty.

Obstruction

Q Your ball comes to rest next to a hut?

A This is an immovable obstruction, find the nearest point of relief and drop the ball back into play within two club lengths no nearer the hole. No penalty shots to be added to your score.

Water hazard

Q Your ball lands in a lake when playing over it?

A Two choices:
1) Drop another ball from where the original was played, or
2) Drop another ball behind the lake and try again. In both cases add on a penalty shot to your score.

Lost ball

Q You lose your ball?

A Play another ball from a position as near as possible to the spot from which the original ball was last played. Add on a penalty shot and remember this is an addition to all shots previously played.

Unplayable lie

Q Your ball is unplayable?

A Three choices:
1) Play another ball from where you played the original, or
2) Pick up your ball and drop it within two club lengths no nearer the hole, or
3) Drop another ball as far back as you like keeping the point where the ball was unplayable and the green you are playing to in line.

In all cases you must add on one penalty shot to all shots previously played.

ETIQUETTE

Pace of Play

In the interest of everyone on the golf course, you should play without delay. If you are constantly slower than players behind, you should wave them through.

73

Out of bounds

Q Your ball goes out of bounds?

A Similar to a lost ball, play another ball from the original spot and add a penalty shot remembering to count all previous shots. **Example –** If your first tee shot goes out of bounds, you tee up another ball and you will now be playing your third shot.

Provisional ball

Q You are unsure if your ball is out of bounds?

A You may play a provisional ball. If you find that your ball is in bounds simply pick up your provisional ball and carry on. No penalty shots.

Winter rules

6"

Q You see a sign saying Preferred Lies, Winter Rules or Clean and Place?

A They all mean the same. In winter the golf course may introduce this above local rule which means you may mark your ball, pick it up, clean it and replace it within 6", no nearer the hole, only on the fairway. No penalty.

74

Casual water

Q Your ball is in a large puddle?

A This is called casual water. You may pick up the ball and drop it at the nearest point of relief no nearer the hole. No penalty shot.

Ball picked up by a dog

Q A dog runs onto the golf course and picks up your ball?

A Just drop another ball where your original ball was and carry on playing. No penalty.

Ball unplayable in a bunker

Q Your ball is unplayable in a bunker?

A Three choices:
1) Replay the shot from where last played, or

2) Drop the ball in the bunker within 2 club lengths, or

3) Drop the ball behind the unplayable shot. But in cases 2 & 3 the ball must be dropped in the bunker.

One shot penalty.

Water hazard

Q Your ball lands in a stream?

A Generally a stream is a lateral water hazard. Drop your ball at the point of entry within 2 club lengths not nearer the hole. One shot penalty.
If you can't find your ball drop another one at the approximate point of entry.

Maximum clubs allowed

Q You have more than the maximum 14 clubs in your bag?

A You must add on two shots to your score for each hole played with more than 14. However if you don't notice the mistake until later in the round the maximum penalty is four shots added to your score.

Embedded (Plugged) rule

Q Your ball is embedded (plugged) in the ground in it's own pitch mark?

A If it's a close mown area (i.e. fairway) you inform your playing partner/s. You may lift the ball, clean it and drop it as near as possible to it's original position not nearer the hole. No penalty.

Taking a drop

Q You have to drop a ball?

A Hold the ball at shoulder height and arms length and drop it.

Ball moves at address

Q Your ball moves after you have addressed it?

A One shot penalty and the ball should be replaced.

Burrowing animal

Q Your ball goes in a rabbit scraping or hole?

A Pick up the ball and drop within one club length no nearer the hole. No penalty.

Andrew's

golf.co.uk

COMPETITIONS

COMPETITIONS

Some competitions and methods
of scoring you need to know

HANDICAPS

A handicap is the number of shots a player may take in addition to the par for the course (see page 64).

What is 'GROSS' and 'NETT'?

GROSS is the total shots you have played on a hole or in a round.
NETT is the score after your handicap has been deducted.

Example:

Your local course may have a par of 70; therefore if you have a handicap of 20 and go round in 90 you have played to your handicap of 20.

Men's handicaps start at 28.

Ladies' handicaps start at 36.

Quite simply, the lower your handicap the better player you are.

The handicap system in golf means that players of different abilities can have a close game.

TIP

For a copy of the rules of golf visit Royal and Ancient website www.randa.org

STROKE PLAY

Peter and Paul go for a game of golf one day.

Peter has a handicap of 12. Paul has a handicap of 20.

Peter takes 84 shots. His handicap is 12 therefore his nett score is 72.

Paul takes 99 shots. His handicap is 20 therefore his nett score is 79.

Peter wins the game.

STABLEFORD

Stableford is a method of scoring that converts your scores into points.

Example:

If your handicap is 18, you will receive a shot on each hole. If you score a 5 on the Par 4 1st hole you have scored a gross 5 minus 1 shot = Nett 4 = 2 points.

Nett score level par = 2 points

Nett score 2 over par = 0 points	Nett score 1 under par = 3 points
Nett score 1 over par = 1 point	Nett score 2 under par = 4 points
	Nett score 3 under par = 5 points

on each hole.

If your handicap is 11 you receive 1 shot on the stroke index holes 1 to 11.
If your handicap is 25 you receive 1 shot on each hole and 2 shots on holes with stroke index 1 to 7.

The person who scores the lowest score on a hole, will have the 'honour' and will play first on the next hole.

If players score the same then the order of play will remain as from the previous tee.

MATCHPLAY

Matchplay is played hole by hole. The lowest score on each hole wins the hole.

The scoring is so many holes 'UP'. The winner being the player who is more holes up than holes left to play.

Example:

Peter is 3 holes up against Paul after 16 holes. Therefore Peter wins the match 3 and 2. (3 holes up and 2 to play).

In the event of the score being level after 18 holes you start again at hole 1 and the first person to win a hole is the winner.

MATCHPLAY USING HANDICAPS

Peter and Paul decide to play matchplay.

Peter's handicap is 12

Paul's handicap is 20

DIFFERENCE BETWEEN HANDICAPS IS 8

Paul receives ¾ of the difference in handicap. The difference is 8, therefore Paul receives 6 shots. Paul takes one shot off his score at each of the 6 hardest holes (lowest 6 stroke index holes). Looking at the score card on the next page, Paul will take one shot off his score at holes 2, 4, 5, 10, 14, 15.

SCORE CARDS

When playing a round of golf with other people using a score card, you would normally swap cards so that someone else marks your card.

As a marker of a card you put your score down in the 'Marker's score' section, and the player's score in Column A.

Name of Competition —————————
Date & Time of Competition —————————
Your Name —————————

The person marking _____
your card's score

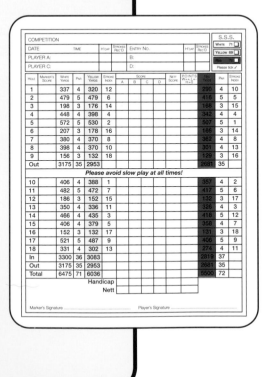

Your total score for ___
second nine holes

Your total gross score —————————

The signature of the person _____
marking your card

Mens Competition Holes

Mens Regular Holes

PAR for the Hole

Mens Stroke index (Difficulty of holes)

Your Handicap

Ladies Holes

The SSS (Standard Scratch Score) is based on the overall length of the course. This is for handicap/competition purposes. Therefore your handicap will be adjusted according to the tees you have played from.

| COMPETITION | | | | | | | | | | S.S.S. | | |

WHITE 71 ☐
YELLOW 69 ☐
RED 72 ☐
Please tick ✓

Ladies Stroke index (Difficulty of holes)

DATE	TIME	H'CAP	STROKES REC'D	ENTRY No.		H'CAP	STROKES REC'D
PLAYER A:				B:			
PLAYER C:				D:			

HOLE	MARKER'S SCORE	WHITE YARDS	PAR	YELLOW YARDS	STROKE INDEX	SCORE A	SCORE B	SCORE C	SCORE D	NETT SCORE	POINTS W=+, L=-, H=0	RED YARDS	PAR	STROKE INDEX
1		337	4	320	12							290	4	10
2		479	5	479	6							416	5	5
3		198	3	176	14							168	3	15
4		448	4	398	4							342	4	4
5		572	5	530	2							507	5	1
6		207	3	178	16							166	3	14
7		380	4	370	8							362	4	8
8		398	4	370	10							301	4	13
9		156	3	132	18							129	3	16
Out		3175	35	2953								2681	35	

Your Scores

Your total score for first nine holes

Please avoid slow play at all times!

10		406	4	388	1							357	4	2
11		482	5	472	7							417	5	6
12		186	3	152	15							132	3	17
13		350	4	336	11							326	4	3
14		466	4	435	3							418	5	12
15		406	4	379	5							358	4	7
16		152	3	132	17							131	3	18
17		521	5	487	9							406	5	9
18		331	4	302	13							274	4	11
In		3300	36	3083								2819	37	
Out		3175	35	2953								2681	35	
Total		6475	71	6036								5500	72	
				Handicap										
				Nett										

Your total score for first nine holes

Your Handicap

Your net score with handicap taken off

Marker's Signature ....   Player's Signature ....

Your Signature

81

Andrew's GOLF
TUITION BOOKS

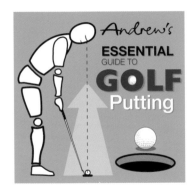

- How to hold a golf club
- How to aim at the target
- The correct posture
- The half swing
- The full swing
- What equipment to buy
- About a golf course
- Basic rules
- How to score and the function of the golf handicap
- About a score card

- The roll of the ball
- How to hold a putter
- The correct posture
- How to aim at the target
- The putting stroke
- How to read a green
- What putters to buy
- About a modern green
- Rules of the putting green

TO FOLLOW
- Pitch and chip like a pro
- Club selection
- Grip position
- How to read the green
- Distance control
- Lob shots
- Chip and run shots
- Recovery shots
- Bunkers in detail
- Rules

Visit www.andrewsgolf.co.uk • Email: info@andrewsgolf.co.uk

For a select range of golf equipment and accessories visit
andrewsgolf.co.uk

Andrew's

golf.co.uk